LOOKING FOR 527

By

Susanne Belcher and Christine Baleshta

Foreward by Katherine Chang Liu and Ron Harton

LOOKING FOR 527
Copyright © 2012 Susanne Belcher/Christine Baleshta

ISBN-13: 978-1467911030
ISBN-10: 1467911038

Artwork by: Susanne Belcher
www.susannebelcherart.com

Essays by: Christine Baleshta
www.wolftracker.com, www.naturewriting.com, www.ylwstone.com

Art photography by: Chuck Buch
Some photographic content in artwork
courtesy of Tim Springer, Photography
www.ylwstone.com

Cover Image:
Looking for 527, 2010, 7 X 6 inches, image transfer collage on paper
Susanne Belcher

Back Cover:
Wolf 527's Radio Collar
Photography courtesy of Tim Springer

Design consultants:
iDivaDesign
www.idivadesign.com

Christina Vogel
canvas29mm@yahoo.com

In memory of Wolf 527F and the Cottonwood Pack

We would like to thank the following for their inspiration,

support, and contributions to this book

Katherine Chang Liu,

Tim Springer,

Camille Belcher,

Ron Harton,

Michael Belcher,

Joan Foster,

Chuck Buch,

Christina Vogel,

and Janet Smith.

PREFACE

In 1996, my husband and I visited Yellowstone National Park - just a year after the introduction of the successful Wolf Restoration Program. Excitement was still in the air throughout the park among visitors and staff alike. Wolves were back and thriving after near extinction and the ecosystem of Yellowstone was being restored in large part because of them.

Then, in April 2009, wolves in Idaho and Montana were removed from the endangered species list and wolf hunts in those states went forward the following September. A month later, a compelling article appeared on the front page of the LA Times recounting the death of Wolf 527F, the much researched iconic alpha female of the Cottonwood Creek Pack. She had been shot and killed by a hunter along with other members of her pack shortly after the coincident opening of Montana's backcountry elk season and the state's first authorized wolf hunt.

I wept. Her story touched me deeply. She had survived in the wild through cunning and intelligence and lived long enough to form her own pack. Somehow, this wolf became both a catalyst for dealing with unresolved personal losses and an archetype for injustices going on in the world today.

As an artist, I felt moved to do something not only to honor this wolf but also to help raise awareness regarding their ongoing plight. While doing some online research, I stumbled upon an essay, written two years earlier, by Christine Baleshta, entitled "Looking for 527". I discovered that she had actually sponsored 527's radio collar and had been tracking "her wolf" for several years during annual visits to Yellowstone. I could only imagine how she felt. I found her website, shared with Tim Springer, a gifted wildlife photographer. I spent hours reading her descriptive, detailed essays and looking at Tim's photos. Her journals about Yellowstone were transporting and made me feel as though I were walking alongside her. This was a person I had to meet. We shared a common passion and I intuitively felt our connection would prove meaningful. I posted on their website and was delighted to receive a response from Christine.

Through subsequent email dialogues that continue today, a kinship was forged and the idea for this collaborative book emerged. It became our vehicle to create a visual tapestry of one wolf's journey and the impact her death had upon two strangers who would become friends because of her.

Susanne Belcher

FOREWORD

ABOUT THE ARTIST *by Katherine Chang Liu, Artist and Independent Curator*

Susanne Belcher looks at the world through the eyes of an artist, but her mind works more like a poet's. Through layers of reduction and compilation of visual information, her images are distilled to form a new whole, reflecting Susanne's central idea. An accomplished and well-established artist, Susanne's language is one of restraint and her images are always compelling.

As a semi-abstract artist, Susanne uses symbolism to suggest her content. Her signature strength is in her versatile and capable combinations of this symbolism in a mixed media of painting, photography and sometimes writing. While her images are both minimal and complex, through the veiled layers we always find a consistent emotional component.

In this series, Susanne's images reflect a core belief that harmony between man and the natural world is necessary; that coexistence flourishes when conditions benefit both, and is at risk when shortsighted policies are aimed towards temporary political gain. Susanne's images are a statement of her deep appreciation for the balance of nature and her concerns that this balance can be easily destroyed when we are not mindful.

Perhaps through the appreciation of the wonder and beauty in Susanne and Christine's work, we will find it necessary to honor the equilibrium between nature and man.

ABOUT THE WRITER *by Ron Harton, Editor, naturewriting.com*

Christine Baleshta has written about the Yellowstone wolves for over a decade, following them through the seasons of their lives. Her writing shows the passion and depth that comes from experiencing life with ones you love. She writes to share that love with others.

Christine writes, not as an objective scientist, but as someone whose heart has been captured by the spirit and beauty of other lives, the wild lives of the wolves. Her words draw readers into those lives so they can experience them with her: the daily life and the big events, the successes and the tragedies.

Her wolf journals read like letters from a friend who is telling the story of what she knows and how she came to know it. For Christine, the world of the wolves is not just something to learn about—it is something to learn from—and she approaches it with admiration and respect. Christine invites readers into the wolves' world and lets them see that they, too, are part of the story, part of the human side of the interconnections of the wilderness world.

It takes courage to write as Christine does, for the wilderness world is assaulted on many fronts. Undaunted by the challenges, she writes with hope for the world she loves.

It Must Be an Illusion

photo transparency collage 8.5x11

she is a four-year-old black female with the Slough Creek Pack. In the picture, she lies in the snow in a drugged stupor, her huge head half-supported by an unseen Wolf Project biologist. Her amber eyes are glazed over and half closed; her pink tongue hangs out the side of her mouth. She has just been re-collared, but will keep her number – 527F. Wolf watchers call her "Bolt" for a Z-like marking on her hindquarters.

LOOKING FOR 527

If anything happens to 527, her collar will be sent to me.

We pass through the Arch on a cold and cloudy May afternoon. Thirteen bighorn ewes graze high above the Boiling River, so many white dots on a blanket of green. At Swan Lake Flats a pair of sandhill cranes feed along the lake shore while geese glide across the quiet surface and elk watch from the hillsides.

Blacktail Deer Plateau lies quiet under the gray of a late afternoon sky. We stop at Hellroaring to look for the Oxbow pups. The Oxbow pack, a spin-off of the Leopold Pack, has made its den

Christine: Thanks so much for your comments and viewing our site. Wish we had other photos of 527, but she was quite illusive and when we did see her...it was usually from far away.

Susanne: I am so thrilled about your response and appreciate anything you can send. The article in the LA Times about 527's death struck such a deep cord in me, I felt moved to do something to honor her.

next to a pond which is visible only through a small window in the trees. They have twelve puppies this first year and the turnout is crowded with people and spotting scopes. Every so often someone spots a tiny black or gray ball of fur, wobbling out of the den and crawling over a log or following one of their adult babysitters.

In the Lamar Valley, a black wolf, maybe a yearling from the Slough Creek Pack, sits under a tree east of the Institute looking from side to side. On April 12, 2006, 527F and the Slough Creek alpha female, 380F, denned on a hillside, but were trapped inside by an unknown pack of twelve wolves from north of the Park, unable to access enough food or water for their pups to survive. Both females have pups again this year, along with possibly two other pack females. We hear that 527 looks good, better than the other Sloughs who are thin, maybe not getting enough to eat. The black wolf gets up, walking into the trees and we lose it.

A pair of coyotes pass Soda Butte Cone and travel toward their den, disappearing in the tall grass. Two years ago we watched coyote

pups here as they played in the sage in front of their den and waited for their parents to bring their dinner. This pair has eight puppies in a different den, but the pups will not emerge until after we're gone. Farther down the road a big black bear forages in the meadows at Warm Springs. He ambles along, close to the road and takes no notice of us. As the sun goes down, the temperature drops. We are back in Yellowstone.

The days drift into a week of cold, clear mornings and warm, sunny afternoons. Bison and elk are everywhere. Each morning more bison calves mysteriously appear clinging to their mothers' sides with bewildered expressions on their red brown faces. The elk are losing their winter coats and growing new velvet covered antlers. Some are scruffy looking while others are so pale they appear almost white. The bison are also shedding, their coats hanging from their backs in pieces of woolly pelts. Soon the elk will have their sleek, brown coats with fluffy white collars and the bison their shiny chocolate colored hides.

As we pass through Lamar Canyon we look for the owl on the south side. The nest is still there, but the owl is gone and in her place sits a red tailed hawk, its head bobbing up and down from the twigs and leaves. Down the road a little further, a fox sits on a large boulder on the north side of the road. He is red-brown with dark slender legs. Someone tells us it's a mountain red fox, a new subspecies of red fox. The fox yawns and scratches himself, then disappears behind the rocks and trees.

We stop at Hellroaring – again – to check on the Oxbow puppies. Two gray wolves are stretched out, sleeping, and another darker wolf walks around nearby, but no puppies. We hike the nearby road that borders the Blacktail Deer Plateau, which is closed to vehicles. Surrounded by snow-capped mountains and only the sound of birds, we spot northern flickers, Clark's nutcrackers, a black and white ladderback, and a warbler

Christine: I think it's wonderful that you want to honor 527. I appreciate correspondence from an artist.

Susanne: Your essay is such a sensitive, poetic piece written in happier times. If you agree, I am considering using fragments of it in my artwork.

Christine: I would be flattered. Your passion has given me the inspiration I needed to get my thoughts about 527 on paper.

Susanne: Attached are scans of some recent pieces. In two, I have incorporated fragments of your essay overlaid with my handwritten thoughts and one of Tim's photos of Lamar Valley.

Christine: I am grateful you contacted me. Your work is beautiful. The first image is stunning – the colors, different placements of her face and the wolf at the bottom add to her mystery. It would make a great cover for "That Book" I might write one day.

Susanne: What a compliment! Ironic that you should mention a book. It was suggested that I consider putting this artwork into book form. I thought of you immediately and wondered if you might be interested in a collaborative venture?

---

with a yellow breast and black markings who flies away too quickly to be identified. The road is dry, imprinted with old coyote, wolf and bear tracks. For all the wolf and bear sign, we have never seen a wolf or a grizzly here.

We sit down to rest on some rocks overlooking a densely wooded area. Below us in a small clearing in the pines a black bear sow plays with her two cubs. The cubs are at least one year old. They roll around in the grass wrestling with each other and pawing their mother. The sow tenderly grabs one and licks its ears. They crawl over the deadfall and climb the slope, disappearing in the pine trees.

Monday morning there are three moose in "Moose Meadow," a cow with her two offspring, one from last year and another from the year before. We see more moose this year, mostly cows with yearlings and young bulls, their budding antlers covered in velvet. Frost covers the swampy meadow, puddles everywhere. Even the smallest moose is big.

Six wolves from the Agate Pack are bedded down in Little America, four gray and

 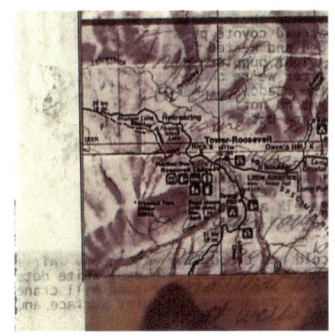 

two blacks. Every now and then, they get up and walk around, licking each others faces and wagging their tails. Two coyotes sit in front of a boulder not far from the Agates, singing and yipping away. We hear them long before we see them. The coyote den is probably nearby and they don't want the Agates around. All the wolves are losing their winter coats, so they appear lighter. The alpha female, 472, is very light with more gray around her face. She is the daughter of 21M and 103F, so she is a Druid, and looks so much like her father, 21M.

The Agate wolves are very mobile and not afraid to cross the road from the South to the North side and back. They go up to Specimen Ridge to return to their Antelope Creek territory, where their pups are waiting for them. This morning we see a wolf cross the road, weave through the sage and disappear. Everyone watches the road, confusing people driving by, but few are lucky enough to see any of the wolves cross.

We check and recheck the Oxbow Pack. Once today we see the alpha female tucked in under the aspens. We don't see the Druids or the Sloughs. The wolves stay close to their den sites this time of year and can be difficult to catch. So we head up the Tower Road to look for Rosie and her two cubs who are one

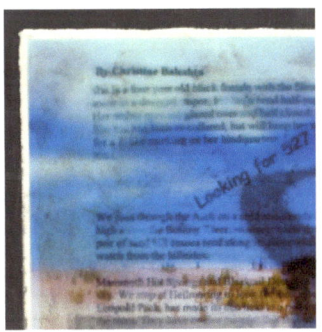  

YELLOWSTONE WOLF PACK TERRITORIES, 2009

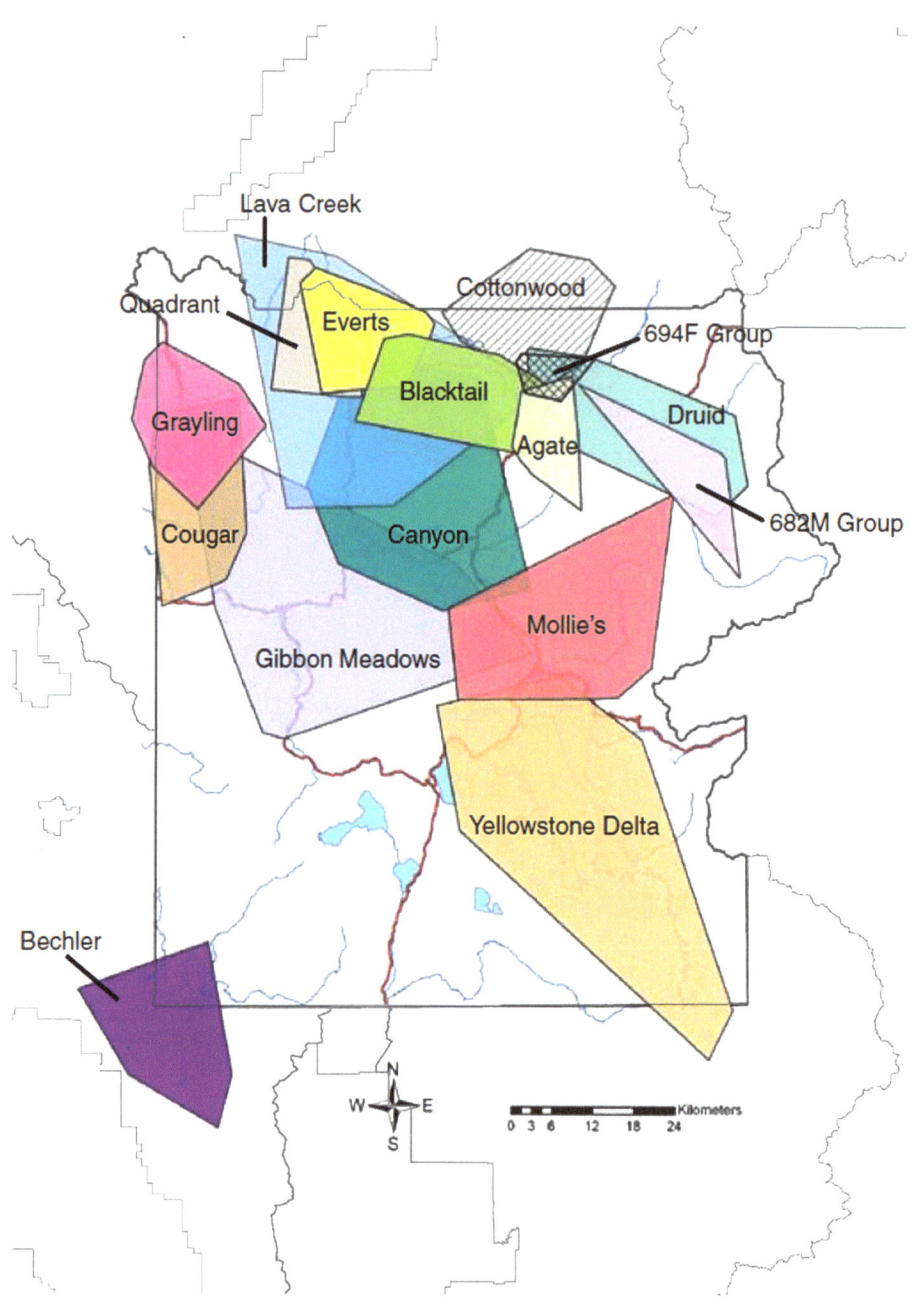

Smith, D.W., D.R. Stahler, E. Albers, R. McIntyre, M. Metz, K. Cassidy, J. Irving, R. Raymond, H. Zaranek, C. Anton, N. Bowersock. 2010. Yellowstone Wolf Project: Annual Report, 2009. National Park Service, Yellowstone Center for Resources, Yellowstone National Park, Wyoming, YCR-2010-06.

year old now. We hike past Calcite where she is almost always nearby. Another couple is climbing the road ahead of us, a sage grouse following closely behind. The grouchy bird nips at the man's heels, protecting his territory. He chases the man away and is not afraid of me as I snap photos. We climb the slope on the north side of the road through the grass and deadfall to a large grassy meadow filled with sage and trees. A wonderful place for bears, but no Rosie. When we return to the road the grouse is gone.

And so the week goes on. We drive to Hayden Valley and get there just in time to see the Hayden Pack's white alpha female swim across the Yellowstone River and lope to the den site, turning her head, tongue hanging out, looking back towards the road. There were rumors that the she had been killed, but she is most certainly alive, healthy looking, and appears to be nursing. The Haydens denned late this year and during the winter were seen exploring Mammoth Hot Springs and Swan Lake. Now they are back in their own valley, a very visible pack.

The Haydens were feeding on a carcass in Alum Creek, something we have seen them do before. The alpha male and a subordinate, also very light gray wolves, cross the road and stop at the river. The subordinate tests the water, looking back at the alpha male. The yearling swims smoothly across and shakes off under the trees on the opposite shore. The alpha male looks stuffed and reluctant to cross just yet. He curls up in the sand and goes to sleep. The yearling waits for the alpha male to follow, but finally beds down behind trees and rocks, out of sight.

Later Tim and I hike part of the Mary Mountain Trail, not far from where we watched the Haydens. The path is wet and we negotiate mud and marshy terrain as it leads us back to a beautiful part of the valley, stretching into more winding creeks and rolling hills, filled with the scent of sage and pine.

Hiking back to the road we notice the Hayden subordinate at the carcass again. By the time we race down the trail and get to the site, he is leaving the carcass. He carries a piece to a spot along the creek where ravens harass him as he tries to eat. He then crosses the meadows to the same trail we hiked. The Haydens often follow this alternate route and cross at the Chittendale Bridge to return to their den when they are unable to cross the road. That is exactly what he seems to be doing when we later spot him up the road.

The southern part of the Park near Canyon and Lake Yellowstone is colder, with snow still on the ground in large patches and steep drifts. Both Yellowstone and Sylvan Lakes are frozen. On Yellowstone Lake, long, thin sheets of ice float on the surface of the water. It feels very remote and looks as if spring has not come here yet. We try to hike Pelican Creek Trail, but it's closed due to bear activity. We walk in as far as the trail signs and stop where it opens to a lovely, oval shaped meadow. Beautiful here. I would like to go back.

Returning to Silvergate we run into a bear jam in Swan Lake Flats. A line of cars and people are watching a grizzly mother and cub try to cross the road. The cub stands up in the middle of the road and looks around and then both bears climb trees trying to get away from the crowd. Unable to avoid people with cameras pressing toward them, the bears move further into the meadow to grub and dig. The mother bear is smart and tolerates humans so well, we believe she might be the daughter of 264, a Park favorite who raised her cubs in this area several years ago.

Hellroaring Overlook is not crowded tonight and we get a good view of the den site. We wait for what seems like forever and are about to give up when seven puppies emerge from the den one or two at a time. The puppies are tiny, but through the spotting scope, their shapes and colors are very clear. Two light colored adults are babysitting the black and gray puppies as they crawl over logs and roll and fight with each other.

Entering the Lamar Valley we catch sight of three wolves on the north side of the road trotting east from Coyote toward the ridge line – two blacks and a gray. They are probably from the Slough Creek Pack, but disappear before we can identify them. I wonder if one was 527.

It is July now and I'm back in Austin, but each day my mind travels an unseen path back to Yellowstone. The Haydens have five puppies, three dark gray, one very light gray, and a black! A yearling female, who we did not see, apparently had pups along with the alpha female. The Druids, spied from a plane over Cache Creek, have four to six, as do the Sloughs, carefully hidden in a wooded area. The Agates are frequently seen at their rendezvous site near Mt. Washburn tending to their eight new members, six gray and two black. There are lots of bears this year, both grizzlies and black, with cubs of the year and one-year-olds. The coyote pups at Soda Butte along with the Hayden Pack pups are the hit of the Park. As I travel back and forth through hot summer days I wish myself there now imagining all the babies.

I think about 527, a mother again. She has been seen frequently since we left, swimming the Lamar River, feeding on a carcass, bedded down in the trees. She does not like the crowds this one and waits till nightfall to cross the road and run back to the den. It's good to know she's safe. Maybe some morning or evening on the next trip I'll be standing near one of her familiar places at just the right moment and look out across the river and the black wolf I see crossing the bench will be 527.

Dark Search
mixed media on canvas 24x40

Path of Ancestral Memories
mixed media on canvas 24x40

I Know She's Out There…Somewhere

mixed media transparency collage on canvas 14x11

If Only I Knew Where to Look

mixed media transparency collage on canvas 14x11

She's on the Move Again

mixed media transparency collage on canvas 14x11

Saying Goodbye to 527

mixed media transparency collage on canvas 14x11

She Must Be Heading North
transparency collage 8.5x11

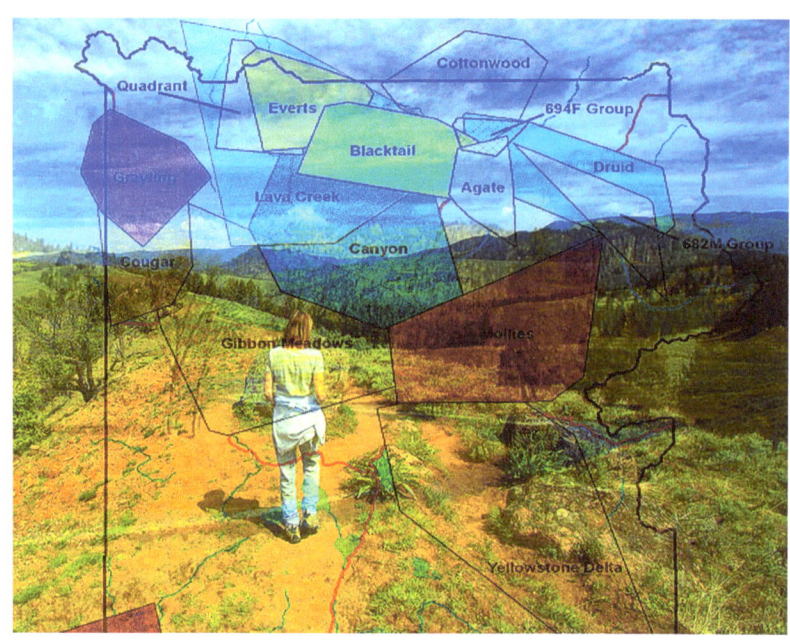

In the Eyes of the Wolf
photo transparency collage
on paper and film 8.5x11

Trip Report - Day 7, June 12, 2009

The Cottonwood Pack is on the basalt cliffs this morning across from Wrecker feeding on a carcass. Six adults, two black, including 716 F, and four gray. 716F was formerly known as the Dark Female in the Slough Creek Pack. Sort of on the fringe of that pack, she has found a home with 527F's pack. Apparently, one of the grays is new, or had not been noticed before, because Rick was remarking about it this morning. The alpha male is gray and uncollared while only 716F and 527F are collared. 527 is not there - she is back at the den with the puppies. I was really hoping to see her this time as alpha of her own pack with her own puppies. At seven years old, I've heard she is starting to gray.

Cottonwood Creek Pack Territorial Grid

collage on mattboard 12x12

Legacy Grid for 527F

collage on mattboard 12x12

On the way to Mammoth we stop where I can look across miles to the opposite hills of Hellroaring. I am searching for 527's den site. The acres of grass and trees and rocks are so vast it seems impossible to find- unless one knows exactly where to look. I don't. It begins to rain and suddenly turns much colder. I haven't seen 527 in about three years. The last time was at a carcass with the other Slough Creek wolves near Aspen one rainy October morning. She has puppies now. Four? Five? Ever the illusive one, she is an old fashioned wolf who shuns the crowds, protects her territory and stays away from other packs. I hoped I would see her this time - just once.

Playing Hide and Seek
mixed media collage on canvas 12x12

Hidden From View
collage on altered paper 11x9

EPILOGUE

I am trying to remember the last time I saw 527. It was a cold, damp, gray October morning and the Slough Creek Pack had a carcass at the edge of the creek, west of the grove of Aspens that stands near the road. The trees stood like yellow bursts of flame, their trunks starkly black and white against the cloudy morning.

Two gray wolves played on the rocks at the edge of the water while a group of black wolves, 527F and 380F among them, tugged at the carcass and carried bones into the scree or rested on the bench. She was so close then. 527 had just been re-collared the previous winter and Tim and I were so excited to sponsor her collar, giddy as new parents.

After that our sightings of 527 were few and she was always far away. She drifted away from the Sloughs and hung around Mom's Ridge and Wrecker and Hellroaring. She met "new" uncollared wolves and they made forays back into Buffalo Plateau. They became the Cottonwood Pack, a group of 5 adults, including a young black wolf, 716, also called the Dark Female, who happened to be 527F's daughter. By the spring of 2009, 527 had pups and the Cottonwoods were thriving. Avoiding other packs, the Cottonwoods traveled between Hellroaring, the old Slough den site and the edge of Lamar Valley. After all the bad years of litters dying and no litters and interpack conflicts, 527 had done very well indeed – she had survived.

In June 2009, we watched the Cottonwood Pack feed on the remains of a carcass on the hills above Wrecker. There were now 6 wolves - 4 gray and 2 black. We watched, our eyes glued to 527 as she stepped over rocks and logs, chased ravens and nibbled at the carcass. And then the next day we learned that it was not 527 at all, but 716. 527's signal had been detected in the same place the day before as she traveled between the den and the carcass – it was even speculated that 527 had made the kill by herself. She had eluded us once again.

And then she was gone. Shot by a hunter on October 3 in Montana's first wolf hunt. 716 went first and then three more Cottonwoods – Yellowstone wolves killed in a wolf hunt. I always believed I would see her again. Each trip we looked for her, searching the hills, driving back and forth through Little America, stopping and waiting at Slough Creek, Wrecker and Hellroaring. I knew she wouldn't live forever, but I never dreamed she would be taken from us like that.

I wondered how I would feel being in Yellowstone on the anniversary of 527's death. No one mentioned her, though Montana's first wolf hunt is far from forgotten. Still, there is something to be happy about. All the wolf packs in the northern range have pups, are healthy and are staying out of each other's way. The best news of all is that the Cottonwood Pack, 527's pack, still exists. They are five wolves, including one of 527's pups and a female called Dull Bar, one of the last surviving Druid wolves, and that is something hopeful to hang on to.

CHRONOLOGY

January 1995 — 14 wolves from Canada released in Yellowstone National Park.

January 1996 — Original Druid Peak Pack wolves are captured in British Columbia and released in Yellowstone National Park.

Spring 2002 — 527F is born into the Druid Peak Pack. Her parents are 42F and 21M.

Spring 2003 — 527F joins her sister 217F, alpha female of the Slough Creek Pack.

Spring 2005 — 716F is born into the Slough Creek Pack and survives distemper.

Spring 2006 — Unknown Pack holds Slough Creek Pack mothers (380F and 527F) and pups hostage; Slough Creek Pack loses all its pups. 527F and 380F survive.

Fall 2007 — 527F disperses and is seen traveling with B271M; 527F's group forms.

Winter 2008 — 527F is seen with a large uncollared gray male.

February 2009 — 527F's group 5 wolves including 527F, alpha female, gray alpha male, 716F (a/k/a "Dark Female), a black male and a gray male, is officially named the "Cottonwood Pack."

April 2009 — U.S. Fish & Wildlife removes ESA protections from wolves in Montana and Idaho.

May 2009 — Cottonwoods have at least 3 puppies.

September 24, 2009 — 716F is shot in Montana's first wolf hunt. The alpha male and one other Cottonwood wolf are killed around the same time.

October 3, 2009 — 527 is killed by a hunter at the edge of Buffalo Plateau. Four Cottonwood Pack wolves remain.

August 2010 — U. S. District Judge Donald Molloy reinstates ESA protections for Montana and Idaho wolves. Wolf hunts in those states are canceled.

October 2010 — Five wolves are seen in the Hellroaring area. They are believed to be 527F's pup, the remaining Cottonwood adults and Dull Bar, a female from the Druid Pack.

POSTSCRIPT

By the end of 2009, the Yellowstone wolf population was down 23% from previous years. The packs in the northern range, which included the Druid Peak Pack, the Agate Pack, the Cottonwood Pack and the Blacktail Plateau Pack, declined by 29%. The famous Druid Peak Pack dissolved in late 2009 and early 2010, mostly due to severe mange contracted by all its members. The Blacktail Plateau Pack lost its alpha male, 302M, a former Druid, who was killed by wolves from another pack in October 2009.

Ruling on a lawsuit filed by several conservation groups, U.S. District Judge Donald Molloy reinstated ESA protections for wolves in Montana and Idaho in August 2010, and wolf hunts in both states were cancelled. In April 2011, Congress, in an unprecedented move, approved the removal of wolves in Montana and Idaho from the endangered species list with language inserted into the 2011 budget bill by Senator Jon Tester, D-Montana and Representative Mike Simpson, R-Idaho. Although the rider was challenged in U.S. District Court by wildlife conservation groups, it was reluctantly upheld by Judge Molloy who wrote "the way in which Congress acted in trying to achieve a debatable policy change by attaching a rider to the (2011 budget) is a tearing away, an undermining and a disrespect for the fundamental idea of the rule of law."

Wolf hunts continued in Montana and Idaho that year killing one Yellowstone wolf, 642F of the Agate Pack. U.S. Fish and Wildlife finally approved Wyoming's wolf management plan in October 2012 allowing them to be shot on sight in most of the state. What seemed like a stream of slaughter of Yellowstone Park wolves began. In November, seven Yellowstone wolves, including 754M, the beta male from the Lamar Canyon Pack, and 823F, a Mollie wolf seen with the newly formed Junction Butte Pack and the only collared wolf in that pack, were legally shot just outside Park boundaries. Then, perhaps most painfully, 832F, called '06 for the year she was born, the alpha female of the Lamar Canyon Pack, was killed in December leaving a huge void in the Lamar Valley. Yellowstone Park wolves, followed by wolf watchers and Park visitors, studied by researchers for years – gone. It was as if hunters were waiting at the Park boundary for them.

Wolf hunts were reinstated to control wolf populations in Montana, Idaho and Wyoming and reduce depredation on livestock. But these Yellowstone wolves, like 527F, were hardly "troublemakers" and left the Park rarely, staying inside its boundaries 95% of the time. Now, as each year the wolf population declines inside the Park, we ask how do we sustain their numbers and solve the conflicts between hunters, ranchers and wildlife conservationists, so that future generations can have that golden opportunity of seeing a wolf in the wild?

For more information about wolves in Yellowstone National Park, please contact the Yellowstone Park Foundation, 222 East Main Street, Suite 301, Bozeman, Montana 59715 www.ypf.org.

Looking for 527

image transfer collage on paper 7x6

BIOGRAPHIES

SUSANNE BELCHER, a native Californian and award-winning artist, found her artistic passion over twenty years ago painting bold and colorful abstract southwest landscapes in oil and watercolor. Although she still considers herself a painter, she now incorporates paint with collage, photography, printmaking and more recently, transparency film. A former health care professional, Susanne has a doctorate in Psychology, is an ardent nature lover, and is an active member of Women Painters West, Collage Artists of America, Valley Watercolor Society, and the Fine Arts Club of Pasadena. Her work has been exhibited in Germany, and shown in several galleries throughout the greater Los Angeles area, and is held in private and corporate collections throughout the United States and Europe. Susanne currently resides in Los Angeles with her husband Michael and their two cats Princess Ruby and Charlie Brown.

CHRISTINE BALESHTA grew up in New Jersey and moved to Texas after graduating from college. An avid journalist, her love of the outdoors and wildlife developed into an interest in nature writing. In March 1994, a close friend gave Christine a wolf hybrid puppy and she became a strong supporter of wolf recovery. Christine took her first trip to Yellowstone National Park in the fall of 1998, and has returned every year since. Her essays and journal excerpts have appeared in wolftracker.com, naturewriting.com ("The Yellowstone Series"), and Yellowstone Experiences (www.ylwstone.com).

www.ingramcontent.com/pod-product-compliance
Lightning Source LLC
Chambersburg PA
CBHW041533280526
45792CB00004B/1489